WILD HEART

A poetry collection by Wingless Dreamer

Edited by

Katie Moino

Wingless Dreamer

UPLIFTING WRITERS AND ARTISTS THROUGH OUR CREATIVE COMMUNITY

Thank you so much for all your efforts and support that you gave to me in past few months. I'm very happy to receive the book as it is my first time when my poem got published and I want thought to show my gratitude to you through this mail. Hope we get to work together again in the future and wishing you all the best for future endeavours.- Mitali Prasad

I'm literally in tears right now, oh my God. Thanks you @winglessdreamerlit !! The books arrived and are AMAZINGLY FANTASTIC! The cover art is beautiful, the collections stunning! I am filled with such surprise and honor my pieces were published with you, it makes me the happiest lassie in the world. Thank you so much!! If you want to support on of the best publishers EVER, go to Winglessdreamer.com or search their books on Amazon! So grateful. -Gratia Serpento

Hi there, I just wanted to say that after reading some of the poetry on Wingless Dreamer, I feel inspired and in awe. I've been writing on and off as a hobby for a few years now but seeing what you've done and how you've built this whole community of writers, I'm really inspired and impressed. You've given me just a bit more inspiration to keep working on my projects and for that I thank you.- Ryan

Best of afternoons! I am simply sending this email to first thank you for this as I am truly humbled by your decision to accept this poem for publication. I wrote this poem after many nights of night terrors and panic attacks due to my looming anxiety over the pandemic and instant changes the world is going through seemingly overnight. Your validation of this poem is received by such validation and a feeling of triumph that I cannot put into words, so genuinely, thank you. -Arnaldo Batista

I am most excited to receive this new book, and I have already shared your various publications with many friends and family! I am very happy to have come across your publication and look forward to reading many more of your other contributor's pieces!- Natalie Kormos

I shall be anxiously awaiting the book's arrival. I always appreciate your editing efforts. They have always been terrific in the past. More book graphics sounds great, I'm excited to see what they are all about. I'm going to your website now and check out what else you have going on, I know you always have a lot going on. You folks are a great publisher in my book, and I'm not just saying that because you've published some of my work, I sincerely mean it and my family and friends agree. Keep up the great work that you do, I know you will.-William David

Keep up this excellent work. Poetry truly connects the readers with poetic souls across countries and cultures – Amita Sanghvi

It is a great joy for me that a kindhearted editor of a journal like you has liked my poem. Thank you again. Be happy in life this is my heartfelt wishes to you.-Sandip Saha

There is such a positive vibes from Wingless Dreamer, unlike any other publisher. -Gavin Bourke

It's an honor and a privilege to be part of the most eminent Literary Journal of the young minds 'Wingless Dreamer.' This is a place where dreams becomes reality. Wingless Dreamer has made possible for all poets & readers to flap the wings of dreams, imagination & aspiration into the deep blue sky of peace, progress & prosperity. You may prosper like the locket of Apollo. You may win unnumbered hearts of poet lovers in future. – Mr. Saheb SK

WILD HEART

Edited and Compiled by

Katie Moino

ABOUT US

In 2019, Indian author Ruchi Acharya dreamed of a literary community that could bridge the gap between fellow, emerging writers with a fervent passion to create and the world of traditional publishing. She envisioned a place where writers and artists are allowed to publish based solely on the merit of their creative skills. Her desire and inspired vision culminated in the design of Wingless Dreamer Publisher, a forum providing aspiring and experienced creators alike the opportunity to share their love of English literature and art on a global platform.

Throughout the year, our Wingless Dreamer team offers a multitude of themed writing contests designed to stimulate fresh ideas and present an opportunity for talented authors worldwide to contribute perspectives through creative expression efforts. We select the best of the best submissions and stream together the components of writing, editing, and illustrating to result in publications of beautiful literary anthologies that we promote in the marketplace. Our commitment to providing this single platform and process allows our authors and artists to bypass challenges and obstacles associated with the traditional publishing goal, and instead maintain their focus and devotion to creating works of art.

Most meaningful is that Wingless Dreamer community members become part of a family, and are guided, encouraged, and supported as they take each step toward cultivating a successful writing or art career. Non-native English-speaking authors are also granted access to free reviews, critiques, marketing, and, in some cases, funding for their work. Our community has slowly, but steadily, grown to become a prominent stage featuring well-known professional writers and artists from all over the world.

Finally, we at Wingless Dreamer are devoted to publishing poetry, fiction, and artwork reflecting the entirety of multiple perspectives and varied experiences extracted from the deep well of soulful human existence. As such, BIPOC, LGBTQ, disabled, minority, and other marginalized voices are especially invited to join in the sharing. Our ultimate goal is to uplift the human spirit through a diverse creative community. At its core, the human spirit desires connections through expressions. We ardently endeavor to gift wings to these heartfelt dreams.

FOUNDER'S PEN

Being a writer can sometimes be solitary and quiet. A writer can understand how it feels to fall in love with every single character, battle with dialogues, work with vivid poetic devices, endeavor for perfection, and build an entire universe from scratch. Guess what? You're not alone. We understand the efforts you put every day into your work. Since we are a team of writers and artists too.

The writing industry is always considered as something obscure and profound by the public in general. It has become so difficult to stand alone and to stick with a writing career in the commercial society we live in today. Compared to other financial and economic-related jobs, things related to writing are the minority.

Writing is a terrific passion, and writers work in a hard industry, one where success is often sought and little received. Writing is not merely something we do, but something we are, and that makes it one of the most challenging of all pursuits in life.

I never got the right support to become a writer at the prime youth of my life. In the place where I come from writing is considered a cute hobby instead of passion - a commitment that writers made to themselves. Writers don't receive the same respect that other professions do. It's quite condescending. That sort of mentality is also so harmful to amateur writers' confidence. From my past experience, I realize that this issue needs to be addressed.

People need to understand that writing is a hard business. It is time-consuming and after dedicating late-night hours, a roller coaster of emotions to finally produce a piece of literary work that might be read around the globe.

So, I come up with this publishing company and yeah I am proud of it.

In the end, I would like to urge all the people who are reading this to never ever give up on your dreams. Seize the day. Every day counts. I hope you will support us and encourage our team efforts. More power to your pen. Cheers! -*Ruchi Acharya, Wingless Dreamer Founder*

JUDGE'S MESSAGE

Thank you to everyone who submitted to this contest. It has been such an honor getting to read all of your amazing poetry. Each poem really has the feeling that humanity is a part of nature, rather than a separate entity. It was wonderful and refreshing to see such unique ideas and creative imagery. It just goes to show how much can be learned from stepping outside and being curious about what we see in the sky, in the garden, or walking down the street. A big congratulations to our winner, runner-ups, finalists, and everyone who contributed to this anthology. I hope you never lose touch with your wild hearts. And if you ever feel that inspiration is hard to find, (we all get stuck sometimes), don't forget to go outside and take it all in.

Katie Moino

ABOUT THE JUDGE, KATIE MOINO

Katie Moino is a poet from Vermont, USA. She's been writing poetry for 20 years now, since age 6. Katie earned her BA in English, Creative Writing from the University of Vermont. Her poems have appeared in Wingless Dreamer's *Dulce Poetica* anthology and Poet's Choice *Attitude of Gratitude* anthology. More to come.

CONTENT

45.	FLEUR	LILY MAYO	80
46.	IT'S SUMMER IN IOWA	JOANNE LEE	82
47.	HER ORANGE CRAYON	SOPHIA FALCO	84
48.	27789	MILKAILA N. ADAMS	85
49.	ROE V. WADE (TWO BIRDS WITH ONE STONE)	DOUG PROFITT	86
50.	DESERT WILDFLOWERS	WILLIAM DAVID	87

🏆 - Grand winner of the Wingless Dreamer Wild Heart Contest 2023

🏆 - First runner-up 🏆 - Second runner-up ⚜ - Top Finalists

Believe in yourself

"I want to use this opportunity to thank all the participants and Wingless Dreamer team to make this publication possible. Every poet has unstained spirit and spotless soulfulness that rests at their very center. Embrace it. Thanks for your support and always remember,

Never give up on your dreams."

–Ruchi Acharya, Wingless Dreamer Founder

1. THINGS TO DO WHEN STUCK INSIDE A CLOSED
DAFFODIL

Guess how many petals will unfold.
Rub up against the pistil. Let it turn you on.
Feel sunshine on your face before your face is even born.
Thirst until your spine shakes and you feel yourself
greening from the inside. Imagine
what wind tastes like. How it is
to be picked and plucked and placed
as the centrepiece. Until you wither
to your death. Quickly. Try to enjoy it. Listen
for sounds within yourself. Be in awe
that you can drink light——
        Be less human, more daffodil.
Consider how people are waiting
to watch you bloom, longing
for yellow. Trust your own radiance.
You have waited all winter. Be patient.
Tell stories about the shadowed soil
from which you have grown. By the time
this daffodil opens, you won't be able to resist
your own flowering. Release your essence.
Stay with the swaying stem of possibility. Imagine
waking slowly to the ones you love. Imagine
all the faces and bright corona crowns
pollinating the landscape with effortless joy.
        Bow to that Earth holding you up.

Guess how many petals will unfold.
Rub up against the pistil. Let it turn you on.
Feel sunshine on your face before your face is
even born.
-Heather Young

HEATHER YOUNG

Heather Mackay Young is a poet, healer and graduate of The Glasgow School of Art. Her writing has been published by Poet Lore, Hummingbird Press, and Olney Magazine. In 2022 she co-created an exhibition called Alchemy, a collaborative conversation about paint, poetry and place with artist Rebecca Styles. She is the 2023 Anne-Marie Oomen Literary Fellow at Poetry Forge. Heather lives and writes on the Isle of Lewis in Scotland where she works toward the restoration of a land based poetics rooted in the unwritten histories of her ancestors.

2. ***

summer is a mystery
the winter of nuclear war still
lives in the heart

MYKYTA RYZHYKH

Mykyta Ryzhykh is a poet from Ukraine (Nova Kakhovka City). Winner of the international competition «Art Against Drugs», bronze medalist of the festival Chestnut House, laureate of the literary competition named after Tyutyunnik. Long list of awards Lyceum, Twelve, awards named after Dragomoshchenko.

3. THE THORNS AND THEIR ROSE

I once grew flowers I never knew
were for the graves of my breaking.
I choked at the world's nakedness and
buried me self in the breath of books,
grinded between metaphors and touch,
humming silent armatures into the
construing ears of earth's sanity.
Time flew past in her arms, feathered
black of flesh and wind and all her breath
I carried so late they tasted as my tongue
sniffing around the teeth denied of language,
and lines and highways of lost poems
that smelled of morning dew trickling
and washing our shadows from falling
on each other on this walkway.

OLADEJO ABDULLAH FERANMI

Oladejo Abdullah Feranmi is a Poet, writer, and veterinary medicine student from Ibadan, Nigeria. A Haikuist, he reads submissions at Sea glass literary magazine and edits for the incognito press. His works are published in Gone Lawn, Hooligan Magazine, The Lumiere Review, and more. He tweets from; @oaferanmi_

4. MYCELIA

a new thing grows in my chest.

weightless roots
waitlists, routes
guest lists
list, guessed;
exchanges change.

a moment, just, to rest
to rearrange the angles, branching shoots,
innumerable fingers, touching, test;
membranes remember, mirror.

touched just right
all things are permeable.

folded self in self,
warm, snug and damp
will split its shell -
seed sprouts, unfurls

gentle through the loam
tracks a fractal grip
drinks a thousand sips
round a stem that lifts
a verdant crown above a home.

gentle through the loam
tracks a fractal grip
drinks a thousand sips
round a stem that lifts
a verdant crown above a home.
-Crystal Eidson

CRYSTAL EIDSON

C.V. Eidson is a lifelong Chicagoan who lives with a devoted husband, two dogs and a serpent. She pays the bills with a succession of low-level office jobs and spends her spare energy creating whatever she can.

5. WAITING FOR CHERRY BLOSSOMS

I visited Japan for the sake of pleasure,
But ended up sick and confined to a solitary retreat,
With only leisure in view,
A solitary cherry blossom tree.

My thoughts were unlike Johnsy in "The Last Leaf",
For I wished to not die in a foreign land,
Where none would shed tears on my tomb.

I wished to return home,
Before I closed my eyes forever.
And so I strived against the Grim Reaper,
Who loomed over my head with burning scythe.

But as days crawled by, I lost all hope,
All my thoughts were extinguished but for one,
To see chrysanthemums before I died.

When I first set foot on this land,
Even though no one greeted me,
I was filled with sheer delight,
For I beheld a truly lovely sight.
Cherry blossoms in full bloom, pale and white,
In stark contrast to the shadow of night.

One day I woke up well before dawn,
To see the sky in a red hue,
People around me cried and wailed,
I was alive while thousands were dead.

Blood spewed and splattered the walls,
It seemed as if the very sun had fallen,
And razed the backs of men with heat.

People their eyes melted,
Stared at me with hollow sockets.

I fainted promptly and while I slept,
Many lost lives around my bedstead.

When I regained consciousness,
I was restored to my former vigour,
Late that summer I boarded the ship back home,
Saved from the clutch of the death.

That year, in Japan, cherry blossoms never bloomed,
It was the bombs that fell instead.

MANASVINI RANGANATHAN

Manasvini Ranganathan is a legal professional working in the social sector in Bangalore, India. Manasvini is passionate about the environment, gender rights, and enjoys exploring intersections between Law and literature in their writing. To reach out for collaborations or discussions: Instagram handle: @manasranganathan, Twitter handle: @manasranga

6. LATE WINTER PUDDLE

The rain
      would make
           a mirror
               of the hole.
The storm
      and snows
           must stop
               first though
                    awhile
and day
      return
          or a great
             moon come out
for you
      and I
        to see
           ourselves
              at all
in the glistening
        riddled
           void
              so full
                 below

JAMES B. NICOLA

James B. Nicola has seven full-length poetry collections (2014-2022). His poetry and prose have appeared in Wingless Dreamer; the Antioch, Southwest, Green Mountains, and Atlanta Reviews; Rattle; Barrow Street; Tar River; and Poetry East, garnering two Willow Review awards, a Dana Literary award, ten Pushcart nominations, a Best of the Net nom, a Rhysling nom, plus a People's Choice award from Storyteller magazine, for which he feels both stunned and grateful. His theater career culminated in his nonfiction book Playing the Audience, which won a Choice award. He hosts the Hell's Kitchen International Writers' Roundtable at his local library branch in Manhattan: walk-ins welcome.

7. ALL DRAWL, NO HUMOR

The night we buried our solitude in the back yard, we thought it must
be a funeral for the dead.
For how could it possibly return?
When we wore joy, painted and dripping down each of our fingers, like
the juice of an over-ripe fruit
plucked just too late from the confinement of its branches.

It's summer and we're kids again. I am sitting on your floor
surrounded by the pages we used to spell
out our imagination and there are ice cubes clinking in frosted glasses
above our heads. Don't you
remember?

As it turns out, it was buried like a treasure, for safekeeping.
Like it knew that one day we would return with shovels and dirt-caked
nails to uncover that
loneliness
whether we intended to or not.

It's summer and my head is on your shoulder and we are breathing in
the trees like thunder after a
long week without the rain. You tell me there is magic in the air you
breathe. You tell me, take it in
and grow strong with it because you'll need it in the fight to come.
What you search for you can find
hidden in your backyard castles, there's no need to blunt your nails on
stone. Sticks and mud will do
the job just fine.

And that faded patch of grass in my backyard, the one unmarked that
held our solitude, it lurked.
It preyed on the corners of my mind at midnight hours, giggling into
my ear that one day,
when the laughter had faded and the sun had died,
then I would return for it.

It's summer and I am drinking whiskey on the porch, and you are
smoking cigarettes like you can suck
life itself back into you. Every time I open my mouth to tell the stories
that we wrote on your floor a
summer ago, you laugh at me.
Squash down that innocence, you say, all drawl no humor, like you've
forgotten it was yours to begin
with.

I would return dig with broken hands for a solitude we buried back
when it was summer.

It's autumn and I miss you sometimes. I miss the kiss of sun against my
skin and painting worlds onto
our arms in ballpoint pen. Like the hand drawn maps in fallen leaves
across the road, back when
there was magic in the crunch of autumn and hidden in the corners of
your smirking lips.

Only then, I would return.

ANNA QUERICA THOMAS

Anna Querica Thomas is a Hispanic American writer, theatre-maker, and PhD candidate
living in Western Australia. She writes speculative fiction and poetry about found family,
queer romance, and connection in dark times.

8. A WREATH FOR PEONY

My garden once bloomed with innocence,
In petals of pink and white.
But I've found in the years of your absence
None of the peonies seem quite right.

Back in the days when you tended them,
Every stem would reach out to your touch.
I don't know just how you befriended them,
But they do not like me as much.

Their veins used to sing with the sunlight
Their petals open wide in sweet song
A blushing bouquet of embarrassed delight
That sprouted when you came along.

Today, I stand in our garden
Wistfully pulling each stalk.
The basket at my hip is laden
With all of our memories and walks

Each of the peonies is warm and soft
Like goose down and wishes ignored
More fragile are they than love itself,
Worth more pain than I can afford.

Sadness mingles on my tongue with bliss
As I picture your cold-tinged nose
The bittersweet tang of the love I so miss
Haunts me as the cold wind blows.

Unspoken words lie between our twin hearts
As I weave the peonies together
And through the susurration of a thousand pink petals
You tell me to move on and to remember.

As I traipse toward your resting place,
The grass between my toes
I hope you can hear me from your hickory case
Among the headstone rows.

"I miss you," I say as I lay the wreath
On my little Peony's bed.
I tuck the peonies at my sister's feet—
And glimpse a glimmer of peony red.

Looking closer, I see something bloom
Right over Peony's heart:
A small red bud has sprung from her tomb!
It feels like a brand new start.

ELLA ABRAHAM

Ella is an enthusiastic writer from Australia who adores creating prose, poems, and even song lyrics. She enjoys editing and dreams of becoming a professional editor, as well as a published author and an English teacher. She currently owns a popular account on Instagram which provides useful advice, motivation and inspiration for writers and can be found under the username @sincerely_writes.

9. SEASONS

if the gods made anything, it would be the seasons

spring breezes in on a gentle wind,
      scented with rain and blooming wildflowers.
hope sprouts along with the grass
waking people from their wintertime blues
and the warmth of the sun finally   starts
to sink into the earth, awakening her from her winter slumber.
leaves bud on trees as she stretches her limbs.
rain dampens the ground and plants hide
              waiting for the sun to come back
and light their faces.

summer sizzles in as the sun beats mercilessly   on the earth,
drying her and slowly turning the plants   brown.
heat and joy intermingle in the air,
quick breezes pull sighs of relief and cloud cover is worshipped.
heat storms slash lightning and ships sail across bright oceans,
splashing waves and catching fish.

fall comes in with the touch of oncoming death,
leaves changing colors, painting the world in bright splashes
orange, yellow and red.
the world cools,
sweaters cover the goosebumps on our arms and
we warm our hands on cocoa, its steam   swirling
in the sky in front of our faces.
pumpkins decorate porches
and we watch slowly as the world starts to die
and fall back into her deep sleep.

winter flashes through in shocking white,
painting the world with ice and snow,
which glistens in the sun   then
turns to grey, dull slush against the sidewalk.
our faces turn pink from the bite of the wind.

the earth sighs as she sleeps,
setting blizzards and wild winter storms racing across her surface
driven by her breath.
the world dies, and we patiently watch for her to be reborn.

AMBER PIERSON

Amber Pierson (she/her) likes a good cup of coffee and sweets. When she's not writing, you can find her curled up with a good book and adventuring with her son.

10. YELLOW

Yellow is summer
Flowers and sunshine
Brightness and happiness
Fading into the glow of autumn
The yellow golden leaves
Falling, drying, dying
Waiting for the quiet of winter
The cold snow falling
Covering the once crunchy leaves
Taking away their voice
Their mobility
Gluing them firmly down
Taking away
Their newly acquired freedom

LYDIA MILLER

Lydia Miller is a dreamer of dreams and spends most work days as an engineer. Navigating a product's development while words are shifting and forming into poems.

11. FALL

The leaves of maple tree,
Falls on the grey earth.
The time to make her free,
Autumn is taking new birth.

The last rays of Sun,
On the bluish brown roofs.
Like the thunder from wand,
Of Zeus; on the night Monsoon.

The bird rushes to home,
The Orange clouds are on high.
Proserpina starts to roam,
To the world of dark nigh.

The world will be covered,
With white plume of falcon.
Nature will lose its glow,
The winter says anon, anon.

The paper will be filled,
With the verses once again.
The grasshopper will take leave,
To relish the shower of spring rain.

The darkness falls on the heaven,
The light has said farewell.
Though I have been majestically driven
To my work, I have to dwell.

The paper will be filled,
With the verses once again.
The grasshopper will take leave,
To relish the shower of spring rain.

The darkness falls on the heaven,
The light has said farewell.
Though I have been majestically driven
To my work, I have to dwell.
-Tavi Shannyal (Saheb)

TAVI SHANNYAL (SAHEB)

Ms. Saheb Sk is a visionary persona who is an author,editor, keen researcher, short story writer and novelist by passion. She has contributed herself to paint the panoramic picture of the sufferings of "Women Society". She has sought solace in the lap of nature and in her poems the core relationship with nature can easily be seen. Ms. Saheb has composed many poems & short stories which are the blend of Classical and modern thoughts. She is free minded and spends her spare time by listening songs or reading books. Her broad research interests include the Growth & Structure of American English, Globalization of English language, a view towards Greek and Roman Mythology and the influence upon the classical author, Feminism and Culture etc. Follow her on Instagram @tanvi_shannyal

12. HER

The time for keeping quiet has not come
Yet the morning is quiet and calm .
Surrounded by tall and leafy trees
A two-storeyed house stands still .
Here the air is cold at noon .

In the balcony an ashtray
In front of a writer .
He stares at the tip of his pen and
In his lap a manuscript .
Flowers turning brown
in a soon-to-be empty flower vase .

Brushing aside the heaps of fallen leaves
A kid cycling in the front yard at 4:30 pm .

In the evening the kid sits to study .
When the story ends , he asks
His father :
Does the Afghan guy return to kabul ?

DEBOPRATIM DEB

Debopratim Deb is an Indian author who writes in English and Bengali. So far he has one collection of Bengali poems titled ' kafer ' (meaning infidel) published.

13. DEER BURIAL

Outside you are burying a two-headed deer and a lamb; whispering to the dirt with the
bones of a shovel. Your brother wraps a pink ribbon around your neck. He is dipping you in amber and pinning you against the wall.

Look at him, a deer says, he would die for you. He would crawl inside your chest and eat the soft parts of your bones. It's romantic, you tell yourself. It's familial.

To your left is a stage full of only wildlife. A play with stinging nettles and deer and a river that follows you wherever you go. You, the deer, picking figs from fat vines. You, the lamb,
fossilised – embalmed.

GENEVA OAKES

Geneva Oakes (they/them) is a Queer English Literature student.

14. AUTUMN BECKONS

The season of growing has ended.
The leaves have changed
   from green to vivid red, are withered,
   and kite-spin into the breeze.
The morning glories no longer open and shut;
   are half closed and drooping
   like old woman wears her shawl.
Dawn and dusk not so far apart now,
   large orange moon sits on the horizon
   reminding it's harvest time.
Reap what was sown,
   move along,
   and join the great migration.

.

CRYSTAL BARKER

Crystal E. Barker grew up on a farm in the hills of Kentucky. She earned a Bachelor's in Nursing from Berea College and went on to earn her Master's in Nursing at California State University, Los Angeles. She has served Veterans for more than 30 years in the VA Medical Center as a Registered Nurse. She is an award winning poet and her poetry is published in county, state, national and international works. Recently she published her collection of poems with Poet's Choice entitled: "Homelessness Through the Eyes of a Nurse in the City" in the English language and is currently working on translating this volume into Hindi, Farsi, and Spanish.

15. TO THE HILL NEXT TO MY HOME (WRITTEN IN OCTOBER)

Rowed brambles on the hills are gay—
they fancy welcome daylight song;
Come has not winter, so today
they stand with brightness all-along,
along the path to the hilltop's ground
each bend and slope is filled with them;
and filled is too the corner mound
whose columns, the road's border hem.
Here roves not yet, the winter-fog
and cold fever so fit don't scowl,
so dapper lymen's feet now jog
and rests on tree- the immotile owl
The wind now more comfortment has
than what in torrid summer blew;
more bubbly is the sward of grass
and milder than the sleety dew.
The heat of light too gently wraps,
o'er all who on this hill reside;
one still can hear the birdie-flaps
ere they in hiemal season hide!
I'll stroll and breathe in wakeful trance
if stays yearlong such atmosphere;
to preside in its fabled romance
and never return from this sphere.

I'll stroll and breathe in wakeful trance
if stays yearlong such atmosphere;
to preside in its fabled romance
and never return from this sphere.
-Shamik Banerjee

SHAMIK BANERJEE

Shamik Banerjee is a poet and poetry reviewer from the North-Eastern belt of India. He loves taking long strolls and spending time with his family. His deep affection with Solitude and Poetry provides him happiness.

16. AN AUTUMN TANGO

look
autumn runs through the trees unfurling ravished
slightly ashamed
just enough to leave behind her
a confused and frustrated red
I told you
I want to taste you

look
the leaves dance on the deserted streets
the tango of days gone by once seduced
by a wind with cold lips loved for a moment and a bit
and then left on an unfair asphalt
I told you
I want to taste you

look
the colours light up in the vineyard
caressed by a time that's right
played out will be in a horde
and squeezed of life
They'll color our lips with must
I told you
I want to taste you

17. BLUE FLOWERS OF OUR LONGING

you've seen how absences pass through our souls
with all the memories of a lifetime
echoing through our hearts
as the din of winter through the bare branches

an allegoric chariot that carries our past
in accents of red hot iron trough our feelings
until tears flood and freeze in us in cold blue flowers
that's how my absences slide
through the faded seconds of time
like candles melted by longing
and snuffed out by the douter
in the dawn that floods the darkness

cold blue flowers that burn like hot iron
each with its fragrance
with its unique taste
and leave on my face
eyes clear of springs
and a splash
of lost spring

CORA MONICA LICHE

Monica Liche is a talented radio producer, writer, and artist with a passion for the creative arts. Her love for storytelling and the arts is evident in her career as a radio producer, where she is able to bring compelling stories to life through her work. Monica also enjoys expressing herself through various creative outlets such as poetry, prose, drawing, and photography. With an art degree from the National University of Arts in Bucharest, Monica has honed her skills in various mediums, and her work is a testament to her talent and creativity. Monica loves to share her work on social media, and you can find her on Instagram and Facebook at @monicliche. Through her art and her work in radio, Monica inspires others to embrace their creativity and pursue their passions.

18. WINTERLUDE

The hush of a midwinter thaw
heavy and damp
envelops our small corner
in a moment of magical suspense

As if Mother Earth has emptied her lungs

a warm breath

a soft pause

Contemplating before inhaling again

Drawing an icy chill from northerly places
The ones we read about and see photos of
and promise our mothers we will never go to

Pulling it closer as we sleep

A howling wind to rouse us from our chilly slumber
and make us dance on bare toes
across frigid floors
to frost-kissed windows

Revealing that we are not the only ones dancing
Glittering willows bob and sway
showing off their icy frocks
and the creek bubbles beneath a glassy floe
While Juncos and Chickadees
keep time with a song

Content that winter has returned

Revealing that we are not the only ones
dancing
Glittering willows bob and sway
showing off their icy frocks
and the creek bubbles beneath a glassy floe
While Juncos and Chickadees
keep time with a song

Content that winter has returned
-Andrea Hunter

ANDREA HUNTER

Andrea Hunter is a writer currently situated on her wanna-be homestead in the suburbs of Chicago. Her work has appeared in Up the Staircase Quarterly, Fauxmoir Literary Magazine, Sad Girls Club Lit, Shady Grove Literary, and more. Connect with Andrea on Instagram: @andrea.hunter3

19. SEASONAL AFFECT

Again I find myself in wait of sun.
The many days we languish in its wake -
This winter is a long and sullen one.

I cherished it when it had first begun -
The autumn in the leaves, the shadow play -
And then, so quick, again in wait of sun.

Outside my morning window, winter dun
Has perched itself in shades of evergrey -
This winter is a long and sullen one.

And, soon - each new depth not be outdone -
A louring westerly will make its way.
Again I find myself in wait of sun,

In wait of walks along the river's run,
The laughing, languid long into the day -
This winter is a long and sullen one.

Ah, would the skies grow wide, enough to shun
The old conceits, the mildew, cold decay -
'Til then I find myself in wait of sun;
This winter is a long and sullen one.

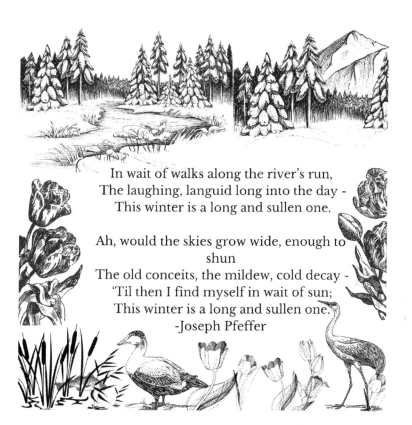

In wait of walks along the river's run,
The laughing, languid long into the day -
This winter is a long and sullen one.

Ah, would the skies grow wide, enough to
shun
The old conceits, the mildew, cold decay -
'Til then I find myself in wait of sun;
This winter is a long and sullen one.
-Joseph Pfeffer

JOSEPH PFEFFER

Joe Pfeffer is a poet, teacher and musician in Sydney's inner west. Accompanied by his wife and two cats, he writes in the quiet moments between grammar lessons and marking essays. His work has been featured in Red Flag Poetry.

20. SURRENDERING TO SPRING

Late winter winds find purpose
in susurring brown-brittled leaves.
Reveal emergent slight green seductions
in remembrance- a form of revival.

Storm-rattled trunks lay down,
sheltering shoots- the next generation;
Keep silent guard under rippling blue skies
as rainbowed blossoms breathe- rhythm is found.

Winter fades as earth makes love
to the clouds – gravid rain bequeathing
legacies of life. Golden sun-sparks light
vital fire- deliver a canvas in verdant array.

Ending gives way to beginning-
Joy the ancestor and posterity of all.

JENNY LARKS

Jenny Snarski – writing creatively as Jenny Larks – is a wife, mother of four and writer living in Northwest Wisconsin. She has lived a life of much discovery, discernment and detours with a perceptive faith and courageous hope. As her children grow, she is engaging opportunities to pursue the craft of poetry and other non-fiction writing initiatives that integrate spirituality, psychology and inspired imaginations with the purpose of helping others find hope, healing and happy endings. Since 2017, she has written for the Catholic Herald, newspaper for the Diocese of Superior. Discover more at www.jennylarks.com.

21. ARIES NEW MOON

Dark and deep and nearly healed
—But I hear her singing me out of the Earth again
Come out! she calls. Together we'll grow!
I have no history and no reason to stay
In one green impulse, I break through the soil

ANN POWELL

Ann Powell is an astrologer based in the desert southwest.

22. BLOSSOM

Delicate as ageing skin
lining springtime boughs
in floods of floral virginity,
arms of innocence,
untouched, unreachable
(except for the breeze)
bloom bountifully, reaching –
high –
for sun rays,
breathing fauna richness.

Apple, plum and pear
creep from green shelters
like soldiers from trenches
in melancholic March
eager to paint-splat
wintery greys,
blocking prior monotony
with candy-stripe glee
and sugar rush highs.

Cherry, blackthorn, hawthorn
weave palette pathways,
stitching arterial limbs:
coursing new life
runs from hedges, scrubland
to fancier, elysian plains
where excitement beats
as hearts of runaway lovers,
casting lines apart
from damning disapproval.

I search for blossom...
scanning tree lines
for fine down

as fledgling feathers;
awaiting small white flowers:
unravelling swans
grown from signets
embroidered by hands of time.

Blossom curls around my finger
as a promise;
curlicues of peony-pink
skip from late May branches,
giggling girlishly
as chains form like daisies
forging floral sisterhoods.

EMMA WELLS

Emma is a mother and English teacher. She has poetry published with various literary journals and magazines. She enjoys writing flash fiction and short stories also. Emma won Wingless Dreamer's Bird Poetry Contest of 2022 and her short story entitled 'Virginia Creeper' was selected as a winning title by WriteFluence Singles Contest in 2021. Her first novel is entitled Shelley's Sisterhood which is due to be published in May 2023.

23. PERENNIAL PETALS

purple flowers line a jagged spiral,
asymmetric and off-center,
not quite a fairy ring
but proof of life all the same-
with a stump in the center
waiting when inspiration lulls.

grape hyacinths they call them,
(grape flowers to me,
penned by my childhood)
used in a six-year-old's
cooking show,
alongside pinecones and wild
Strawberries.

violet bulbs hang homemade fairy cups,
delicate and layered,
used to pour out Spring
and proof of life all at once-
with empty space in their centers
waiting until inspiration flows
once again.

EMILY NEWBY

Emily Newby is a twenty-one-year-old student and poet from Broken Arrow, Oklahoma.
In 2020, she attained first prize in the Tulsa City-County Library's narrative essay contest
and, in that same year, earned honorable mentions for poetry and short stories in the 16th
Annual R. Darryl Fisher Creative Writing Contest. Her work takes inspiration from a
childhood spent in nature and the struggles of new adulthood.

24. BOILED FLOWER

Have you ever placed a flower into a boiling pot of hot water?
How about a rose?—a rose of astounding colors. Yellow, orange, pink, and red;
Oh my! A wizarding rose of beautiful bountiful bloom.

If you place the rose in whole—stem and all—the flower blooms!
Faster.
Yes, that means the flowers shed faster, falling ever so gently into a beautiful stew;
Get rid of the stem. You don't need that. You have to let loose sometime.
Just consider it a greening growing grass that doesn't need mowing anymore.

No, no more blooming isn't bad. Thinking of it like a dog happily let loose off its leash,
Running with a merry little leap over a sunflower patch—a glow you can't deny.
When it bubbles, think of it as a wonderful change about to happen.
You want it.
Think of it like going independent—a flower aiming to be sterling strong and slippery.
Think of it like being as happy as you can be.

So shed your rose's leaves—change is not going going gone. It's just as welcoming
As you want it to be. Besides roses are strong, and if you didn't want to boil it just yet,
And it bloomed to fast, too soon. Don't worry too much.

At least it'll make a fantastic reddening realistic rose tea.

S

So shed your rose's leaves—change is not
going going gone. It's just as welcoming
As you want it to be. Besides roses are strong,
and if you didn't want to boil it just yet,
And it bloomed to fast, too soon. Don't worry
too much.

At least it'll make a fantastic reddening
realistic rose tea.
-Kaylee Stull

KAYLEE STULL

When not teaching, Kaylee Stull is writing horror, sci-fi, and poetry. An absolute horror fanatic, she grew up reading and telling stories about ghosts, monsters, and anything psychological. She is from Northern California and attended Cal State Long Beach where she obtained two BA's in English Creative Writing and Literature. In her spare time, she hones her archery skills. Her social media links are: Kitkatstull (Instagram) and Kitkatstull (Twitter).

25. AN ODE TO OUR APARAJITA (THE PIGEON WINGS BLUE FLOWER)

Fair Mistress of my garden,
your blue adornment astounds e'en the skies.
My mother, the house-warden,
when sees you, there's refulgence in her eyes.

More clear your hue than all be:
on Summer, when a lake does blue attain;
in April, the Nupur tree;
before dawn, midair's sapphire yon the main.

You are called the Pigeon wings;
because you match a Culver's flaps and tail;
for all idoneous things,
you are the mascot who to us avail.

Your bluish magnificence,
makes you the fame-born flower of this place;
and your vernal florescence,
is like the brightness on an infant's face.

Your mid has patch of White,
the Blue surrounds it like planets to Sun.
I have seen you are more bright
than the irised sky when rain is done.

You talk with: Drongos, Sparrows,
Bridewort, Crape Jasmine and Periwinkle;
with birds: of seed sand burrows;
with flowers: of day's sunlight and star's twinkle.

You are sentiments' envoy——
when you hue's the lightest, you make us ease;
You are the passional joy,
that gives a bard his poetry and peace.

You are bluest on the day
when mother collects you with feet unshod;
then you're the holy nosegay
with which she glorifies our temple's God.

SHAMIK BANERJEE

Shamik Banerjee is a poet and poetry reviewer from the North-Eastern belt of India. He loves taking long strolls and spending time with his family. His deep affection with Solitude and Poetry provides him happiness.

26. TULIPS RISING

Eager anticipation of spring's tulips rising
Solemnities a slightly ironical rainbow of blooms
Hymns to heavenly noisy church flower vases
Meadows of murmuring waters harmonizing
Unmentionables full of scrutinizing petals
Shadow less early morning philosophical garden crawl
Gun-whale of her boat full of butterflies
Stuck in the mud last fall
Smelling fresh printed rag paper from Budapest
As she unwraps her Roses
Darkness shining in the brightness of the Baby's breath
At the Nurse's Station
Shadow lay over the rock under the Iris
Bristles shining wirily in the weak light

TERRY BRINKMAN

Terry has been painting for over forty five years, has five Amazon e-books, and poems in Rue Scribe, Tiny Seed. Winamop, Snapdragon Journal, Poets Choice, Adelaide Magazine, Variant, the Writing Disorder, Ink Pantry, In Parentheses, Ariel Chat, New Ulster, Glove, and in Pamp-le-mousse, North Dakota Quarterly, Barzakh, Urban Arts, Wingless Dreamer, LKMNDS and Elavation.

27. ON A RAINY SPRING DAY

on a rainy spring day,
the flowers drink up
and the air is filled with the
thick sweet smell of happy verbena flowers
the mockingbirds sing
through the damp air
and the melody blends with the ring of my ears,
a consequence of the late night behind me,
the sun finally emerges from behind heavy clouds
to beam on the lake
and create soft shimmering waves,
like the aura that surrounds a fire when it burns too intensely,
i easily become lost in the golden haze
as i watch small critters tussle for an acorn
the rainy spring day
makes my peace feel reborn

KATHRYN O'NEILL

Kathryn O'Neill is a poet/ writer based in Texas. Her work touches on themes of growing up, nature, relationships and more.

28. WINDSWEPT DAFFODILS

Windswept Daffodils
Southern belle yell-ow bonnets
Gripped tight by green stems

SARAH MUNOZ

Sarah Munoz is from Roanoke, Virginia. She is a mother, a secondary English teacher, and a poet. She writes in various styles; however, introspective poems have always come naturally to her. Sarah's poetry has appeared in Wilderness House Literary Review, New Reader Magazine, Mythos Poets Society (Mythopoets), blood moon Poetry, and The Roanoke Times, among others. Her Instagram handle is @ponderpoet.sarah.

29. HIBISCUS FLOWER

She rests now
In a warm grave
Her song, quiet
The wind bends
Without her soft melodic tune
That carried a gentle voice
Unscathed by her circumstances
Her struggle, ever-present
But not in her music
It was made
By the purist parts of her
And like the red Hibiscus flower
She once wore in her brown hair
It bloomed
Her joy-
Fragrant,
Yet bittersweet
Like the rigorous ups and downs
Of her life
And in death
We leave Hibiscus flowers
On her grave
And when the wind
Ruffles their petals
You can hear her voice
Singing softly in the breeze

She rests now
In a warm grave
Her song, quiet
The wind bends
Without her soft melodic tune
That carried a gentle voice
Unscathed by her circumstances
Her struggle, ever-present
But not in her music

-Monica Viera

MONICA VIERA

Monica Viera is a Latinx author from East LA.

30. SPRING OUTSIDE THE CITY

Laying in the bed of myrtle, and playing checkers with the rabbit
In the backyard of my aunt's house
Blowing kisses at the mourning doves
Daffodils in my dark hair, like Kore's crown
I'm alive out here
In the early April sun and first rain
Morning strolls down by the creek
Writing love letters to the Lord of Spring
Like I'm a girl again
I feel reborn, the trees budding and blossoming
And I'm a nursing a chickadee to full health
Like my mother, in a swing and me at her breast
What goes around comes around
And we all fall back in love with heaven's baby breath
Soil under our nails and open curtains in my bedroom
May air tastes so sweet

AURORA MONTEJO

Aurora Montejo is a university student studying Creative Writing. She's a cat person and avid romance reader.

31. IN BLOOM

Red and some near-perfect pink
impatiens sprinkle throughout
the backyard path.
Entering,
The unmistakable overwhelming
scent of peonies cascades from across the garden
Filling your nose with the
pleasaunce of beauty
emulsified.

Daffodils belay their heavy heads
On their stems
Swaying rhythmically-
systemically
in the wind.

The blooming shoots of lilies
pry open entropically,
stare at the sky existentially;
Pollen laden in the air.
White daisies shoot up
still green on the inside, with
fans of white
like the sun.

Fresh baby-pink roses in a gentle bush
lie waiting to burst in
little firework clusters
I had tried to clump them together,
I never knew they craved space.

The seeds I have planted today
Are the flowers I will enjoy tomorrow.

Fresh baby-pink roses in a gentle bush
lie waiting to burst in
little firework clusters
I had tried to clump them together,
I never knew they craved space.

The seeds I have planted today
Are the flowers I will enjoy tomorrow.

-Michelle Walsh

MICHELLE WALSH

Michelle Walsh is a poet and pharmacy technician studying Creative Writing and her pharmacy interest at the University of Iowa. You can find her on social media @alotoanxiety

32. APRIL 1998

I put a chair between houses in back,
spring detailed in sun-infused air.
Heat feels like life and now here, I am life.
Vines sworl, tiny-leafed and new green.
Puffed sparrows dart round about me.
Weeds wave in the cracks of bricks.
Grace flows in me and all I see.

GINA OLIVIER

Gina Olivier is an attorney and judicial law clerk in New Orleans. Gina studied literature as an undergraduate at Tulane University. She lives with her husband Richard, daughter Rachel and dog Aly.

33. SPRING NIGHT SOPRANOS

The dusk-chorus ceremonially releases the night
As the last blackbird puts down his instrument
Frogs, taking up the mantle, sing-in the pink moon
Spawning over their differences.
Sculpted dainty translucent wings take to the sky
To perform their nightly airborne operetta,
A spot-lit conductor snatches stardust from moonbeams
Meticulously clearing the stage
Of an effervescent entomology.
Twitch-snitching bullrush fluffed-reeds
Crackle and pop the caldron pot-pond
Hot with life, in inky-cold silvered waters;
The treeline's barely-budding bird-filled backdrop
Belies a sticheron's notation
Tucked-up highline woodpigeon – a treble-clef.
Precocious slumbering daffodils accent indigo-ed-greens,
Pronouncing the anticipation of a verdant ecstasy
Darkly readying a renaissance of audacious spectacle;
Subterranean worlds plotting their domination
Quietly germinating opportunism and loosening hardened soils.
A ruminating and impatient agitation,
Seeding silent battles of resource-capturing encroachment.

LELIA SLIM

Leila Slim LLB LLM is a British writer of Palestinian-Greek/Scottish-Canadian heritage brought up and in Athens, Fife Scotland and London England, currently living and writing in Athens. Leila's work has so far featured in Popshot 2020 Protest Issue, The Caterpillar 2021 Spring Issue, and will be featuring in a book being published by Duke University Press in 2023. Leila was recently the winner of the Wingless Dreamer 'Open Theme' poetry contest with a poem of hers featured in their Cradle of Balladry compilation.

34. SHAKESPEARE'S SAFFRON

Perchance to dream
Of intersections tween flowers and figures
Discover the fault in no stars
Of six-fold inscribed petal precision
      Give every man the voice
      Requesting the spice
      Give fewer still
      The ear to hear the price demanded
How far the candle throws a beam
Casting light upon the toil
For the robbed steals from the thief
Paid in sweat equity for each stigma taken
      For what is begun cannot be unstarted
      So little a single flower yields
      Though each may be small
      The flavor to savor is fierce
One touch of the spice makes all equally kin
Yet one pound requires the world to reap
For even Horatio finds the ratio
Not worth the effort if not worth the excess
      No treasure for inaction
      No time to stare at a beauty within
      Now purple with profit presumed
      As seen like Henry to Boleyn
Such as saffron is made
Such as saffron can be
All the world is this spice's stage
Where all must agree

No treasure for inaction
No time to stare at a beauty within
Now purple with profit presumed
As seen like Henry to Boleyn
Such as saffron is made
Such as saffron can be
All the world is this spice's stage
Where all must agree

-Andy Betz

ANDY BETZ

Andy Betz has tutored and taught in excess of 40 years, lives in 1974, and has been married for 30 years. His works are found everywhere a search engine operates.

35. THE FINAL OPIATE

> *. . . the opiate of the people.*
> —*Karl Marx*

As poets kept on writing about flowers
and felt important, graduate degrees
helped mindful persons fill the fading hours.

Some lavished lovers stepping out of showers
so shimmeringly, you'd tremble at the knees
and feel their love, as fragrant as their flowers.

The modern state, to exercise its powers,
decided to rescind tuition fees
for mindful persons if they filled their hours

with poems; there were hidden penalties
for muckraking—or muck—or grist that scours
corruption. We kept writing about flowers,

us, beauty, love, and personalities.
The slightest sting of social conscience sours
the sauce, we learned. It takes a person hours

to overcome: much prettier to please.
Some cast in dungeons dark or tallish towers,
some exiled, those who would not smoke the flowers
went unheard, even through the final hours.

us, beauty, love, and personalities.
The slightest sting of social conscience sours
the sauce, we learned. It takes a person hours

to overcome: much prettier to please.
Some cast in dungeons dark or tallish towers,
some exiled, those who would not smokethe
flowers
went unheard, even through the final hours.
-James B Nicola

JAMES B. NICOLA

James B. Nicola has seven full-length poetry collections (2014-2022). His poetry and prose have appeared in Wingless Dreamer; the Antioch, Southwest, Green Mountains, and Atlanta Reviews; Rattle; Barrow Street; Tar River; and Poetry East, garnering two Willow Review awards, a Dana Literary award, ten Pushcart nominations, a Best of the Net nom, a Rhysling nom, plus a People's Choice award from Storyteller magazine, for which he feels both stunned and grateful. His theater career culminated in his nonfiction book Playing the Audience, which won a Choice award. He hosts the Hell's Kitchen International Writers' Roundtable at his local library branch in Manhattan: walk-ins welcome.

36. IF I WAVE I CAN'T UNWAVE

I don't wave hi anymore because what use do I have for another petal
that waves bye.
So now, the violets whisper hi
and greet me with their bodies.
With eyes closed, I can still see
that the gray sky is an empty page–a reset.
Because looking is an expensive transaction.
And the only thing I eat are rainbows.
They say there's no i in team, but there's an i in family.
So I remind myself that even light wants to hide sometimes.

FRANKIE LEE

Frankie Lee delivers food and works in a library. Originally from southern California, he
and his family now live in northern California.

37. THE JOYS OF SPRING

Spring's photodump: Long fingers
of wild lavender. Confetti trails
of blossom petals. Wildflowers
crowning the earth. Daffodils,
always the daffodils, brightening
their surroundings with buttery light.

And, don't forget, lambs, lambs,
lambs. Chocolate eggs melting
quicker than an Easter sandcastle
left to the tides.

Summer, meanwhile, waits in the wings.
Practises turning sunsets pink
with every sip of a strawberry
margarita.

CHRISTIAN WARD

Christian Ward is a UK-based writer who has recently appeared in Dodging the Rain, Blue Unicorn, The Seventh Quarry, Bluepepper, Tipton Poetry Journal, The Amazine and Rye Whiskey Review.

38. GRATEFUL BLOSSOM

The spring rain
showers desert's floor,
so precious in this dry land
measured in 100ths of an inch.
Yet this small amount
is just enough
for cacti's annual bloom.
A blossom opens—
nectar's sweet scent
wafts on gentle breeze
summoning the pollinators.
Angel white petals,
star shaped, delicate and soft
are landing pads
for bees to make way
to her center with long stamen,
full of fluffy golden pollen
that they carefully gather onto
barbed hind legs.
She hums joyfully,
in tune with their buzz
as the wind
brushes her softly.
Gaze upturned
at the open blue sky,
she basks in the glory
of three gifted days on this earth.
Then, her ending nigh,
poised on the green arm of her mother,
she clasps her petals
and bows her head
in a prayer of gratitude
for being a part
of this great circle of life.

Then, her ending nigh,
poised on the green arm of her mother,
she clasps her petals
and bows her head
in a prayer of gratitude
for being a part
of this great circle of life.
-Crystal E Barker

CRYSTAL BARKER

Crystal E. Barker grew up on a farm in the hills of Kentucky. She earned a Bachelor's in Nursing from Berea College and went on to earn her Master's in Nursing at California State University, Los Angeles. She has served Veterans for more than 30 years in the VA Medical Center as a Registered Nurse. She is an award winning poet and her poetry is published in county, state, national and international works. Recently she published her collection of poems with Poet's Choice entitled: "Homelessness Through the Eyes of a Nurse in the City" in the English language and is currently working on translating this volume into Hindi, Farsi, and Spanish.

39. A GIFT FROM MOTHER NATURE

I look up into the sky,
Around me birds sing sweet melodies,
Rays of light from the sun warm my skin,
Fresh grass below me tickles my feet.

A mosaic is how I would describe the beauty of the sky,
Each cloud unique from the other,
And modest enough to let the sun peak through with her bright beauty.

My favorite color was that pale sky blue from the moment I saw it,
Birds, dragonflies, bees, and butterflies flew across Mother Nature's
backdrop every so often,
Each part played a role in what I loved so much about the sky,
Each cloud, each insect, and each sun ray come together to be a
masterpiece of nature's
artwork.

KELSEY TRAN

Kelsey Erica Tran is an aspiring young poet. She graduated as the Senior Speaker-Class of 2022 at her high school. Kelsey uses her voice to bring attention to topics she's passionate about like being Asian American, disabled, and a young woman. Find her @boredlittlescorpio on Instagram.

40. CARNATION

Resides in turf by the brook.
Dew evaporates from verdures.
In summer shade, it may be overlooked.
Outspreading in daybreak's allure.

It's fringed, scarlet pads mollifying.
Extends their petals to the water's edge.
Vines continue skimming and ossifying.
Will not, for a moment, be dredged.

Piquant incense from the center——profusion.
Further augmenting the sense of seclusion.

RICHELLE BRUNSTETTER

Richelle Brunstetter lives in the Pacific Northwest and developed a desire to write when she took creative writing in high school. After enrolling in college classes, her overall experience enticed her to become a writer, and she wants to implement what she's learned into her stories. Just starting her writing career, her first published story appears in The Beloved Christmas Quilt beside her grandmother, Wanda E. Brunstetter, and her mother, Jean. Richelle enjoys traveling to different places, her favorite being Kauai, Hawaii.

41. PECULIAR PARTICLES

the sun caresses the few
      f r e c k l e s on my face, that we both share
twin signatures – signed by the heavens,
      sending sunbeams to darken the **ink**

I bury my feet in the sand,
and the peculiar particles comfort my entire body,
like how it felt to have you hold
my hand when we crossed
the street from the group home to the 7-Eleven

the seafoam looks fluffy
      and inviting, like the whipped cream
on the blueberry Jell-0
      they served us in the visitation area
on your birthday, but sadly
      it also the thought of you returning, it is merely a façade

It turns out to be a turbulent and arduous
massacre of the living,
concocting a foul-smelling froth that coats the shallows.

The sweet solar sigil turns to a burning
bully, a benign branding
of your brash behaviors.

What was once warm and comforting between my toes,
is now course and cold; all of this accomplished
with an attempt to get closer to the truth.

Never fully letting go
despite my attempts, just like your impact and influence.
The peculiar particles attach to me, sticking to every part they touch.

Leaving it all behind – a seemingly impossible task.
It permeated my life and found
its way into every
crevice
it
could
fit.

Weeks later, in my pockets
when I reached for the coins, I found
at the bus stop in front of the soup kitchen.

Months later, when I cleaned out my closet
and found the shells that I forced
myself to not remember collecting.

Years later, when I opened my backpack after a long trip
to visit my adopted family;
a few particles would always make themselves known.

every time I thought I had gotten rid
of these peculiar particles,
I found them hidden in some place I forgot

you never explained
why your memory shares so many characteristics with the sand
nobody wants it around, making a mess of things

What was once warm and comforting
between my toes,
is now course and cold,
all of this accomplished
with an attempt to get closer to the truth.
-Steven Sandage

STEVEN SANDAGE

Steven Sandage is a poet based in Visalia, California. He began writing poetry in his early teens. Poetry allowed him the freedom to express himself without limits. He is majoring in Creative Writing at Fresno State University. His projected graduation year is 2024.

42. MISTY HILLS

Mind as misty as the hills I tread,
Is it vulnerability that I must trade?
The waterfalls do orchestrate,
And so do the streams,
Let time, carve its own course,
In its own sweet pace.
For now it's monsoon,
Mindless and yet a mind of its own,
Clouded, shrouded and in its tempest,
But the winter shall soon serenade with serenity,
And streams turn as sapphire as the sky,
While the rowdy waterfalls turn to whisper.
And the Cherry Blossoms paint the promenades pink,
Maybe just trudge on till then to think.
But for now, make peace with the charade,
that the monsoon brings.

SOMDEEP DATTA

Somdeep hails from the city of Kolkata, India. A person of varied interests, Somdeep has a passion for travel, writing and photography. He has experiences working with travel blogs, college tabloids, magazines and publishing. Somdeep is an Engineering graduate with background of Computer Science and is currently working in an IT role for the Government. Somdeep considers wordplay and satire as the sharpest arrows in his quiver.

43. A TIME OF CHANGE

(for Asa Marie)

Summer stretched long and bountiful
bright smiles and strawberry memories
sun-kissed lilacs and irises
lifted our spirits for awhile
newly-plucked blueberry smoothies
the sharp sweet smell of fresh-cut grass
smoke and sparks rising from the grill
formed a false sense of permanence

For as the sun's rays wane
lignon berries replace
their indigo sisters
lilies of the valley
wither into heather
earth's wool-woven sweater

While cherishing summer memories
we fondly look ahead

TS S. FULK

TS S. Fulk, a neurodiverse English teacher and textbook author, lives with his neurodiverse family in Sweden. After getting an M.A. in English literature from the University of Toronto, he taught English in Prague, CZ before settling down in Sweden. Besides teaching and writing, TS S. Fulk is an active musician playing bass trombone, the Appalachian mountain dulcimer and the Swedish bumblebee dulcimer (hummel). His poetry has been (or will be) published by numerous presses including The Light Ekphrastic, The Button Eye Review, The Fairy Tale Magazine, Journ-E, The Red Ogre Review, Perennial Press, Lovecraftiana and Wingless Dreamer. Instagram: @tssfulk_poet www.island-of-wak-wak.com

44. LILAC CORONATION

I have always felt like
A kingdom could flourish
Within the boughs of
A fragrant blooming lilac.

Lords and ladies recline
On four-petaled flowers
As knights march up
And down beshadowed stems.

A maiden spins gold from
The pollen in the center
And there- a dragon nests
Between periwinkle folds.

The aroma of purpled scent
Wafts off like banners
Swaying from the turrets
Of the highest branches.

Medieval romance sprouts
From its heart-shaped leaves
Which cradle raindrops like tears
Falling from unrequited lovers.

The lilac kingdom trumpets
Its call to all of the senses
Beckoning adventurers forth
To the glories of its blossoms.

Medieval romance sprouts
From its heart-shaped leaves
Which cradle raindrops like tears
Falling from unrequited lovers.

The lilac kingdom trumpets
Its call to all of the senses
Beckoning adventurers forth
To the glories of its blossoms.
-Nikolai Razumov

NIKOLAI RAZUMOV

Nikolai Razumov is a fine artist from the Washington D.C. metropolitan area. He is a recent graduate of American University, earning his Bachelor's degree in literature and creative writing. As an artist and aspiring author, Nikolai draws much of his inspiration from nature, mythology, Medieval illumination, and Renaissance drama. He aims to incorporate whimsy and wonder into all of his creative endeavors.

45. FLEUR

Hydrangeas and Lilies

My mother named me after a wildflower in hopes I would always grow. And I've learned a couple of things in the garden, watching her plant kindness and bloom love.

1. Flowers are high maintenance.

Plants need sunlight, and soil, and water, and air to grow.
Flowers can think that they are too much of a hassle, and therefore will refuse to ask for help.
You might have to listen carefully to what they are not saying.
Sometimes, they wilt. Sometimes, they bloom.

2. Talking to flowers increases their growth.

(some people may call you crazy for talking to your houseplants, but in response send them the twelve-dozen articles you have saved in your phone that prove talking to your plants improves their health, and yours.)

Flowers are shy.
Primarily because they are conscious of how high maintenance they are.
They think that their bloom is not worth the wait.
They forget that we need them just as much. They breathe in the air we exhale.
They feel pressure to bloom, so it is best you reassure them that they are enough.
Love your flowers softly. They are delicate wild things.

3. Just because a flower wilts— doesn't mean it's dead.

My mother taught me that flower cycles are cyclical.
Just because a plant withers in the winter doesn't mean it will come back next spring.
It is okay for flowers to weep, because it comes before the bloom.

4.   They will bloom again.

Each blossom, a flower will tell you that their bloom is the best one yet.
(This is growth.)
They will claim this is the happiest they have ever been because
happiness is relative, and they had yet to know it like this.
(This is growth.)
They will look back at their past blossoms and be disgusted by how
they compare.
(This is not growth.)
*Remind them that maybe her petals weren't as vibrant, but goddamn
did they bloom.*

LILY MAYO

Lily Mayo is an aspiring young author. She has loved writing since she learned to hold a pen in her hand. Her work has been published with Beyond Words, Poets Choice, Sepia Quarterly, and more publications can be found on her instagram @lilycatmayo or on lilycatmayo.com.

46. IT'S SUMMER IN IOWA

It's summer in Iowa which means the table's always set & everything smells like asphalt mirages & there's no clouds, only sparse bits of meat-smoke that don't do anything to block the sun & it's just past mating season & for the short-lived things this means everyone is either coming into or out of the world in rotating doors & there's just never a way to be polite in those, is there & in such close quarters animals are nothing if not honest & at home my family starts gathering to eat instead of stopping by like a neighborhood drive-through & the grill is out even though the wood of the deck is old, like the kind of old where the hardware store guy takes one look at the picture and can't even place it on the damage scale & after we eat barbecue straight out of the runny tinfoil I go out onto the deck & my knees are a little soft with fear & the deck goes a little soft too in response & when it creaks I kneel down at the right place between two wooden slats & wipe sweet corn juice off my fingers onto the exposed part of the wood like it's sweat & the pores take it right up like it's ice cold drink & the summer always feels young somehow & makes me think for a moment if I touch my dog I won't feel the hardness of his age & makes me think if I hold my mother she'll be unused, not dusty-sweet like the static pulling off the surface of an analog television screen & I press my face on the line between the two floorboards to see a bundle of newborn robin's chicks in the nest on the support beam underneath & they're lying in cool shadow & I am not their mother, yet they open their mouths for me & somehow it's still too early in their species to be born with a fear of children & I whisper through the floor to warn them of the ones that would scream just to see them startle & I will forget to warn them of the ones that would whisper, the sound only prompting soft beaks to strain open again and again to nothing & I am still a child, I think & I am not my mother, who would leave them be & yet the chicks open their mouths for me still as if trusting I could grow into her & I am not my mother, but one day I'll scoop a nearly grown chick from the lawn back into the nest when it falls, too heavy for its own mother to carry & the summer's door will turn & I'll find that somehow, I'm ready for it.

I think & I am not my mother, who would
leave them be & yet the chicks open their
mouths for me still as if trusting I could grow
into her & I am not my mother, but one day
I'll scoop a nearly grown chick from the lawn
back into the nest when it falls, too heavy for
its own mother to carry & the summer's door
will turn & I'll find that somehow, I'm ready
for it.
-Joanne Lee

JOANNE LEE

Joanne Lee is an undergraduate student studying biology and creative writing. When not writing, she does Lion Dance and plays on her 15 year old Wii.

47. HER ORANGE CRAYON

The orange crayon made the setting
sun possible as he held on to the string
taking him upwards that was made possible
by the birth of creativity, outside the lines
as the string swayed as chaos ensued as the
orange crayon became smaller such force from
a small hand from the will of imagination.

SOPHIA FALCO

Sophia Falco's third poetry book: Chronicles of Cosmic Chaos: In The Fourth Dimension has been published by UnCollected Press 2022. In addition, she is the author of Farewell Clay Dove and The Immortal Sunflower. She is the winner of the Mirabai Prize for Poetry. Falco is in a highly regarded Master of Fine Arts Program for Poetry along with carrying out a Teaching Fellowship to make her dream career become a Professor of Poetry.

48. 27789

In the summer my connection to
The earth
Is immense - the warmth of the sun
Brushing over my shoulders
The heat emanating through the dirt
Beneath my toes
And into the soles of my feet
Living primitively
Off the campsite
With solar panels to power my only connection
To others
I am not bothered by worldly things
In these moments
My only concern is which book
I will read next
As I sit in my rainbow hammock
And watch the river flow

27789 – Pincode of the camp site.

MILKAILA N ADAMS

Mikaila N. Adams is a poet from Hillsborough, North Carolina. She is currently pursuing her B.A in English, Secondary Education at the University of North Carolina at Greensboro. In her free time, she enjoys reading, exploring the outdoors, and collecting antique cameras.

49. ROE V. WADE (TWO BIRDS WITH ONE STONE)

The road is like many you'd see—
especially around these parts;
some here say a road's a road.
But to her, much too familiar;
she knows its winding ways.
The bumps— the forestry:
hogtied-gagged-rolling
around in the back of
a rusty pickup bed.
It kept her awake,
even while nodding, afraid.
Normal attempts at rest
long ago tossed away.
Felt it left her only one choice:
up to us now to be their voice.

DOUG PROFITT

Doug got tired of writing for himself and began submitting, mostly poetry, for publication in 2020. Presently he is compiling his prose and poetry in book form to offer later this year.

50. DESERT WILDFLOWERS

I walked outside into my yard this morning.
A cool morning breeze was gently blowing,
making my good feeling now almost complete.
Looking down, there at my feet,
I saw a small burst of bright orange flowers growing.
Looking around, I could stay here and look for hours.
My eyes took in the different colors of all the wildflowers,
the desert was displaying,
with all its' glory showing.
My feelings, I felt so full, there was no denying.
Their bright beauty set my spirit glowing,
and my inspirations went flying.

I leaned over and picked a few flowers.
A careful collection of all the colors,
the orangest oranges, the brightest yellows,
a few flowers of blue,
a dark brilliant hue.
Some pretty deep purples and little white wild daisies.
I made a multi-colored bouquet,
to my eyes a sight that so pleases,
a gift from nature that really made my day.
I know they all have a specific scientific name,
the likes of which I cannot say,
but I love my lovely desert wildflowers just the same.

WILLIAM DAVID

William David has had a 40+ year career as a Senior Engineering & Architectural Designer working with international mining companies, designing mineral processing plants around the world, including the first SX-EW copper processing plant in Asia, located near Monywa, Myanmar. William is retired now, living with his wife of 39 yrs. in Tucson, Az. He is now devoted to his passion, reviewing, and writing poetry. William writes for his pleasure, and for the pleasure of those who might read his poems. He has been published in three journals by Underwood Press, the flagship journal Underwood, also True Chili, and Rue Scribe journals. He's an invited reviewer for that publisher. His poems have appeared in online journals, Bluing the Blade, Elevation Review and Sheepshead Review. He has had poems published in 19 different anthologies by Wingless Dreamer Publishers. Check them all out on Amazon's Authors Page for William E. David.

WRITE. FEEL. PUBLISH

NEVER GIVE UP ON YOUR DREAMS.

IT'S NEVER TOO LATE

If you liked our work, kindly do give us reviews on Amazon.com/winglessdreamer. It will mean a lot to our editorial team. You can also tag or follow us on social media platforms:

Instagram: @winglessdreamerlit @ruchi_acharya

Facebook: www.facebook.com/winglessdreamer

Mail us: Editor: editor@winglessdreamer.com

Sales: sales@winglessdreamer.com

Website: www.winglessdreamer.com

You can also support our small publishing community through donation:

www.paypal.me/Winglessdreamer

WRITE AND WRITE, AND SET YOURSELF FREE.

BOOKS PUBLISHED BY WINGLESS DREAMER

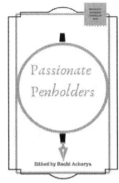

ssionate Penholders   Passionate Penholders II   Art from heart

Daffodils   Father and I   Sunkissed

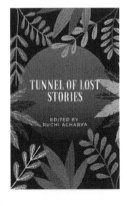

Tunnel of lost stories   Overcoming Fear   The Rewritten

BOOKS PUBLISHED BY WINGLESS DREAMER

Fruits of our quarantine

Magic of motivational

Diversity

Dark Poetry Collection

A glass of wine with Edgar

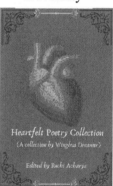

Heartfelt

A tribute to Lord Byron

Wicked young writers

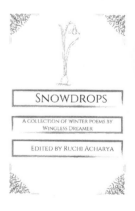

Snowdrops

BOOKS PUBLISHED BY WINGLESS DREAMER

The Wanderlust Within   Writers of tomorrow   BIPOC Issue

 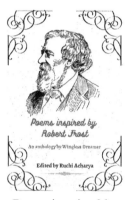 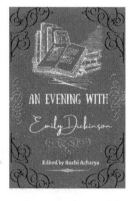

Shakespeare of today   Poem inspired by Robert Frost   An evening with Emily Dickinson

's time to snuggle up   Depths of Summer   Flee to Spring

BOOKS PUBLISHED BY WINGLESS DREAMER

How to stay positive

It's twelve o clock

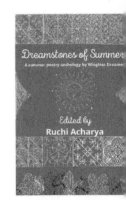

Dreamstones of Sun

Dawn of the day

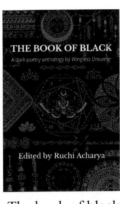

The book of black

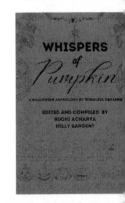

Whispers of Pump

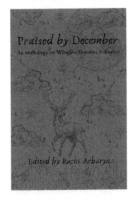

Praised by December

Calling the beginning

Snowflakes and
Mistletoes

BOOKS PUBLISHED BY WINGLESS DREAMER

My Cityline

My Glorious Quill

Garden of poets

Let's begin again

Field of black roses

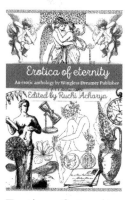

Erotica of eternity

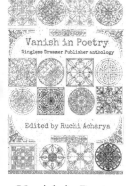

Vanish in Poetry

Oxymorons and Poets

3 Elements
Poetry Review

BOOKS PUBLISHED BY WINGLESS DREAMER

Still I rise

Mother, a title just above queen

Ink the Universe

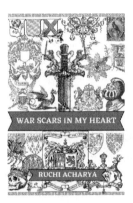

War scars in my heart

The Black Haven

I Have a Dream

Midsummer's Eve

Sea or Seashore

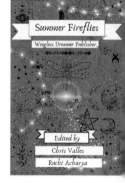

Summer Fireflies

BOOKS PUBLISHED BY WINGLESS DREAMER

Evening, Wine, and Poetry

My Unheard September

Unveil the Memories

Paranormal Whispers

Dulce Poetica

Christmas Cheerios

My Sanskriti in Teal

Wings of Wonder

Growth in Grief

BOOKS PUBLISHED BY WINGLESS DREAMER

  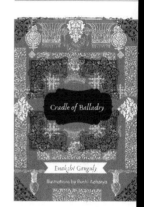

Rhapsodies of Rhyme   Crystalline Whispers   Cradle of Balladry

 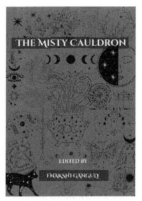 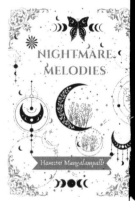

Poetry on Life   The Misty Cauldron   Nightmare Melodies